How Do I Stay Safe From Cyberbullies?

Tricia Yearling

Online Smarts

How Do I Stay Safe from Cyberbullies?

Tricia Yearling

BULLY
FREE
ZONE

E **Enslow Publishing**
101 W. 23rd Street
Suite 240
New York, NY 10011
USA

enslow.com

Words to Know

alias—A made-up name that someone uses to hide his or her real name.

anonymous—Unknown.

block—To stop or slow the actions of others.

chat—A conversation that takes place through instant messaging.

evidence—Facts that prove something.

hosted—Given a home.

identity— The traits that make people who they are.

message board—A Web site where people can read and post messages on a particular topic.

profile—A short description of a person online.

screen shot—A saved copy of what shows up on a computer screen at a certain time.

social network—A Web site where people connect with family and friends.

target—A person who is the object of a bully's attention.

text message—A written message sent by cell phone.

thread—A chain of online messages about a subject.

Contents

What Is a Cyberbully?

You have probably heard about bullying at school or at home. Maybe you know someone who has been bullied. Or maybe you have been the **target** of a bully yourself.

A bully is someone who scares or hurts other people. They try to make their targets feel weak and helpless. Some bullies physically hurt their targets by hitting, slapping, or kicking. These people bully in person. Other bullies use words or pictures to scare their targets. These people

SAFETY TIP!

Only open messages from people you know and never reply to messages from a cyberbully!

can even bully from far away. A cyberbully is someone who sends messages on computers and cell phones to spread fear.

Attacking Online

Cyberbullies use Web sites, **social networks**, and **message boards** to attack other people. For example, these bullies may make hurtful statements or post embarrassing pictures of their targets online to make them feel bad. Understanding how cyberbullies work can help you deal with one.

How It Works

Computers and cell phones help people to stay in touch. This means that your family and friends

Being bullied online can make you feel sad, threatened, or angry even when you are offline.

are always only a few clicks away. It also means that bullies can reach their targets at any time. Cyberbullies can even get to people in their own homes.

There are many ways that cyberbullies can try to reach you. These bullies can send an unwanted e-mail, **text messages**, or **chat**. They may post nasty notes on Instagram or send out mean tweets on Twitter. A cyberbully may even post a story about you that is not true in a place where you cannot delete it. It is difficult walk away from a cyberbully.

SAFETY TIP!

Educate your friends about cyberbullies.

Why People Bully

All bullies, including cyberbullies, intimidate for a reason. They may feel bad about themselves and think that being a bully will make them feel better. They may get bullied by someone else and think that bullying will give them power.

Cyberbullies may think they are **anonymous**. They can choose screen names that hide their **identities**. They can **block** their phone numbers when sending you texts. They may even pretend to be people they are not. Cyberbullies think they will not get caught. However, cyberbullies can be caught. They sometimes get into big trouble for their bullying. Parents, schools, and the government are fighting against cyberbullying.

Unmasking a Cyberbully

If someone you don't know is sending you mean messages, it can be very scary. However, there are ways to figure out who is bullying you.

Pay attention to the words that a cyberbully uses in a message. Bullies often use the same words in person that they use online. Sometimes they will talk about things they have done in person. You may be able to outsmart your cyberbully. When you read a message, ask yourself, "Does this sound like someone I know?"

SAFETY TIP!

Print mean messages and show them to an adult. Then block the sender and delete the message.

Some cyberbullies use their real names. If they think bullying makes them look cool, they might want their friends to know what they are doing. Tell an adult you trust right away if someone is bullying you. Do not feel embarrassed or ashamed. You have done nothing wrong.

Collecting Evidence

Cyberbullies give clues with every message they send. They usually send the same kinds of messages over and over again. With the help of an adult, collect these messages as **evidence** against a bully.

Telling an adult you trust that you are being bullied online can be the first step toward stopping the abuse.

Print out e-mails or messages on your social network from the bully. Forward text messages to an adult's phone. Take a **screen shot** to capture mean or scary things that a cyberbully says in a chat room or on a message board **thread**. Some cyberbullies use several different names. Write down the names of everyone who sends you bullying messages.

Ask for Help

Being the target of a cyberbully hurts. Getting mean messages can make you feel alone. When people write bad things about you on a Web site, it can seem as if the whole world is against you. Remember, you are not alone.

Telling a trusted adult, like a parent, guardian, or teacher, can be a huge step toward stopping cyberbullying. Aunts, uncles, grandparents, and babysitters are also good people to talk to. These

SAFETY TIP!

A cyberbully is usually someone you know. Look for clues in the messages they send.

An adult can help you collect the evidence you need to shut down the cyberbully.

people can help you collect evidence. They can contact a Web site administrator to try to find out who the bully is and to take down mean or untrue stories. A trusted adult can even help you figure out ways to stop the bullying.

Being Safe Online

There are rules on the Internet. Just like at home and in school, it's not a place where people can say and do whatever they want. For example, online message boards have rules about what people can write on them. Using bad words and putting people down is often not allowed. Breaking the rules can get bullies kicked off of Web sites.

There are rules about what people can send by e-mail too. Web sites are **hosted** by companies

Cyberbullying is a problem that people need to work together to solve.

called Internet service providers, or ISPs. In some cases, ISPs can track a user to find out who he or she is. If you get a bullying message, tell an adult. With the evidence you collect, an adult can call or e-mail the ISP and ask the people there to deal with the problem. Tell an adult if someone says that he or she is going to hurt you. The adult may decide to tell the police. You should not feel as though you are in danger when you use the Internet.

Protect Yourself

The best way to stop cyberbullies is to keep them from reaching you. A cyberbully can reach you only if he can find you using technology.

If you use texts, send instant messages, or talk with friends through social networks, you may be online more than you realize. Keep your personal information private when you are online.

If a cyberbully is sending you hurtful messages, tell an adult. That adult can have the phone company block messages from the bully's phone number.

Be careful whom you give your phone number, e-mail address, or **profile** on a social network to. Use an **alias** for your e-mail address and screen name.

If a cyberbully sends you a message, do not reply. Cyberbullies want you to reply. They want to know that they have upset you. Block bullies so that they cannot reach you again. Ask an adult if you need help blocking messages from a particular e-mail address. You can also block numbers from calling your phone. Remember, you have done nothing wrong. It is the cyberbully who may be breaking the law.

SAFETY TIP!

Keep your e-mail address, instant-messaging screen name, and phone numbers private.

★ **25** ★

Don't Be a Cyberbully

○ ○

Being cyberbullied can make you feel helpless. Some targets of cyberbullying may want to bully back or bully someone else. Do not do this. It only makes another cyberbully on the Internet. If you do not know what to do, ask an adult for help.

Treat people the same way online as you treat them in person. You would not yell at someone or say things to scare or embarrass them. Be respectful to people online. Do not type in all capital letters because that is like yelling. Never

By being respectful and friendly in your online messages, you are using good manners.

SAFETY TIP!

Start a Cyberbully Stoppers Club so you and your friends can talk about your experiences on the Internet.

use bad words. Do not send texts or e-mails when you are angry. If you do, people may mistake you for a cyberbully. Everyone online can help stop cyberbullying. Remember this every time you log on or turn on your phone.

Learn More

Books

Kowalski, Robin M., Susan P. Limber, and Patricia W. Agatston. ***Cyberbullying: Bullying in the Digital Age.*** Malden, Mass.: Wiley-Blackwell, 2012.

Minton, Erin. ***Cyberbullies.*** New York: Rosen Publishing, 2014.

Nelson, Drew. ***Dealing with Cyberbullies.*** New York: Gareth Stevens Publishing, 2012.

Schwartz, Heather E. ***Cyberbullying.*** Mankato, Minn.: Capstone Press, 2013.

Truesdell, Ann. ***How to Handle Cyberbullies.*** North Mankato, Minn.: Cherry Lake Publishing, 2013.

Web Sites

cyberbully411.org

Gives tools to deal with cyberbullying. Includes real-life stories of young people who were bullied.

stopcyberbullying.org

Tells how to respond to cyberbullying and how to prevent people from becoming cyberbullies.

Index

Published in 2016 by Enslow Publishing, LLC.
101 W. 23rd Street, Suite 240, New York, NY 10011

Library of Congress Cataloging-in-Publication Data
Yearling, Tricia.
 How do I stay safe from cyberbullies? / Tricia Yearling.
   pages cm. — (Online smarts)
 Audience: Grade 4 to 6.
 Includes bibliographical references and index.
 Summary: "Discusses how kids can protect themselves from cyberbullies"—Provided by publisher.
ISBN 978-0-7660-6851-3 (library binding)
ISBN 978-0-7660-6849-0 (pbk.)
ISBN 978-0-7660-6850-6 (6-pack)
1. Cyberbullying—Juvenile literature. 2. Cyberbullying—Prevention—Juvenile literature. I. Title.
 HV6773.15.C92Y43 2015
 613.6—dc23   2015006992

Printed in the United States of America

To Our Readers: We have done our best to make sure all Web sites in this book were active and appropriate when we went to press. However, the author and the publisher have no control over and assume no liability for the material available on those Web sites or on any Web sites they may link to. Any comments or suggestions can be sent by e-mail to customerservice@enslow.com.

Photo Credits: Cultura RM/Nancy Honey/Collection Mix: Subjects/Getty, p. 28; DrAfter123/Digital Vision Vectors/Getty Images, p. 23; Elena Kalistratova/iStock/Thinkstock (chapter opener and front and back matter); Fuse/Getty Images, p. 9; junpinzon/Shutterstock.com, p. 27; Jupiterimages/Stockbyte/Getty Images, p. 12; Jyotirathod/Digital Vision Vectors/Getty Images, p. 24; Kamira/Shutterstock.com, p. 15; karelnoppe/iStock/Thinkstock (boy), p. 3; Lurin/iStock/Thinkstock (bully free sign), p. 3; MachineHeadz/E+/Getty Images, p. 6; Pat148321/iStock/Thinkstock, p. 5; Purestock/Thinkstock (series logo) p. 3; Rob Marmion/Shtterstock, p. 18; Sashatigar/iStock/Thinkstock (doodle art on contents page and fact boxes); Shouoshu/iStock/Thinkstock (digital background), p. 3; Tony Cordoza/Photographers's Choice/Getty Images, p. 17; Victor Habbick Visions/Science Photo Library/Getty Images, p. 21.

Cover Credits: karelnoppe/iStock/Thinkstock (boy); Lurin/iStock/Thinkstock (bully free sign); Purestock/Thinkstock (series logo); Shouoshu/iStock/Thinkstock (digital background).